The Forward book of poetry
2003

FORWARD
LONDON

First published in Great Britain by
Forward Ltd · 84–86 Regent Street · London W1B 5DD
in association with
Faber and Faber · 3 Queen Square · London WC1N 3AU

ISBN 0 571 21694 3 (paperback)

Compilation copyright © Forward Ltd 2002
Foreword copyright © Michael Donaghy 2002
Front cover image by VV Rouleaux

Reprographics by Vision · Milton Keynes

Printed by Bath Press Ltd
Lower Bristol Road · Bath BA2 3BL · UK

A CIP catalogue reference for this book
is available at the British Library.

To Joseph

Preface

WELCOME TO THE 2003 EDITION of the *Forward book of poetry*.

The world of poetry is a small one, yet the variety, both of poets and of work, is astounding. In this year's collection, alongside such well-established names as Tom Paulin and Peter Porter, we have gifted younger poets whose reputations are still in the making, Clare Pollard, Tom French and Robert Seatter among them. Themes range from the everyday to the mythical, moods are nostalgic or pragmatic, exuberant or regretful, styles energetic, lyrical, haunting, rumbustious... Such variety is the strength of an anthology; its weakness is that it can give only a taste of a writer's work. While many poems do stand alone, others are part of a sequence and can be only fully appreciated when read with their fellows, so do use this collection as a springboard to explore some of the year's most exciting poetry.

As always, the collection been chosen by five extremely dedicated judges to whom we are very grateful – Peter Stothard, former editor of *The Times* and now editor of the *Times Literary Supplement*; Rosie Millard, arts correspondent of the BBC; and three noted poets: Sean O'Brien, Lavinia Greenlaw and, in the chair, Michael Donaghy. They read over a hundred collections and a hundred single poems and I'd like to thank them for all their efforts.

I'd also like to thank the many people and organisations who have helped make the Forward Poetry Prizes and National Poetry Day possible. They include Lesley Miles at Waterstone's, Jeffery Tolman at Tolman Cunard, Gary McKeone and his team at the Arts Council of England, Christina Patterson and her team at The Poetry Society, Dotti Irving, Liz Sich, Truda Spruyt and Sophie Rochester of Colman Getty, our partners at Faber and Faber and the BBC, and everyone at Forward.

I hope you enjoy this latest collection.

William Sieghart

Foreword

POETRY HAD BEEN FILLING OUR FRONT ROOMS since early spring – every other day we seemed to find ourselves signing for another box of slim but suspiciously heavy books until the final count totalled 109 volumes and 104 single poems. And here at last, after months of re-reading, reconsideration, general eyestrain and mild brain damage, is the eleventh *Forward book of poetry*.

Can we say in all honesty that this selection represents all that is best in contemporary British verse? I'm sure the publisher wouldn't expect anyone to swallow such a naive and arrogant assertion. Consider for a moment the effect of arguing literary merit by committee; a committee, moreover, possessed of wildly divergent (but solidly 'mainstream') literary values, a panel which includes the previous year's winner as a matter of policy, a debate in which any one judge's passionately defended first choice can easily be lost in the cut and thrust of an exhausting five-hour negotiating session. Yes, there's room for reform. But poetry prizes – and their attendant shortlists, exclusions, canonisations and journalistic bitchiness – are a necessary part of an open literary culture and, reservations aside, we're all in agreement that our final choices command and reward attention. Yes, hard sacrifices were made, but this anthology should occasion far more celebration than resignation.

We agreed to look for clarity, imaginative daring, a willingness to challenge the reader as well as to meet that reader halfway, and a sense of the integrity of the line (one book-length poem was dropped from discussion when we agreed it was a novella with an unjustified right margin). An art forger once told me that in his field the acquisition of technique is no more than a matter of patient attention. The real difficulty, he explained, is eliminating the contemporaneity of one's taste. Some of the poets we read over the past few months seemed to be engaged in a species of forgery, incorporating all they had absorbed from their reconnaissance of contemporary verse – and nothing else. But we found all the qualities we sought among a broad spectrum of voices ranging from the oneiric to the satiric, the impassioned to the ironic, the political to the intimate, the narrative to the rhetorical.

We all found the Best Collection shortlist the most difficult case. Many eminent established and emerging poets have published highly polished and challenging collections this year. If the permitted shortlist were longer it might well have included brilliant new work by, among others (and to list them in alphabetical, not preferential order), Simon Armitage, Carol Ann Duffy, Geoffrey Hill, Selima Hill, Sarah Maguire, Robert Minhinnick, Alice Oswald, Ruth Padel, Peter Reading and Robin Robertson – all of which I urge you to purchase. As it stands, we have included brief selections from these works in the anthology.

Among the collections that did make it into this category, Auden's influence loomed large. This was due, of course, to an accidental grouping of two or more judges attuned to that frequency. But perhaps Auden epitomises certain values represented by the Forward Prize. Since 1994 William Sieghart has used the Forward Prize and the media attention it commands to bring poetry before an intelligent general readership. The judges are drawn not only from the specialist world of poetry but also from the milieux of journalism and fiction. This would have pleased the author of *Another Time*, who bridged the elliptical high modernist mode with a relatively accessible poetry of intellectual engagement, a public poetry capable of discourse, logic and satire, which could just as easily slip into the visionary, a poetry which could tap into traditional rhythms as well as free verse. This strain is perhaps most explicit in Peter Porter's *Max is Missing* (which features a poem entitled 'Scrawled on Auden's Napkin') and John Fuller's moving and technically accomplished *Now and for a Time*. But a version of Auden is also just detectable in the imaginative energy and formal elegance of Paul Farley's *The Ice Age*. We were also taken by the double nature of David Harsent's *Marriage* – first painterly and intimate, then nightmarish and mythic – and the rich, synaesthetic language of Vona Groarke's *Flight*.

The selection process for Best First Collection wasn't much easier, but we feel sure that Henry Shukman, Julian Turner, Tom French, Stuart Pickford and Chris Considine are all poets set to rise to even greater prominence in the future.

Then it was time to argue the shortlist for the Best Single Poem. The difficulty we had at this stage is reflected in the short count of four finalists. We agreed to admit Jane Draycott's striking description of rowing from her sequence of poems written as part of Southern Arts' RiverWorks residency, together with three elegiac inventions: Medbh McGuckian's encounter with her mother's grief (at least that's our interpretation) in 'She is in the Past, She has this Grace'; Carol Rumens' memory of the pianist Phyllis Robinson in 'The Submerged Cathedral'; and Ian Duhig's evocation of the late Andrew Waterhouse in 'Rosary'.

At the time of publication we haven't yet selected the winners in these categories and I expect our final meeting will be, shall I say, 'lively'. I want to salute my hardworking fellow judges, Rosie Millard, Lavinia Greenlaw, Peter Stothard and Sean O'Brien, for their passion and commitment. And I'm sure they join me in expressing my gratitude to Sophie Rochester and Liz Sich for their patience in dealing with their confused and overworked charges, and to William Sieghart of Forward Publishing for his faith in poetry and its readers.

Michael Donaghy

Publisher Acknowledgements

Ann Alexander · DEAD CAT POEM · *Facing Demons* · Peterloo Poets

Simon Armitage · CHAINSAW VERSUS THE PAMPAS GRASS · *The Universal Home Doctor* · Faber & Faber

Jonathan Asser · LOST IN BAYSWATER · *The Switch* · Donut Press

Caroline Bird · MULTITUDE · *Looking Through Letterboxes* · Carcanet

Colette Bryce · THE WORD · *Poetry Review*

John Burnside · HISTORY · *The Light Trap* · Cape Poetry

Chris Considine · THE CRUELLEST CLASS · THE LAMB AUCTION · *Swaledale Sketchbook* · Smith/Doorstop Books

David Constantine · LEGGER · *Something for the Ghosts* · Bloodaxe Books

Sarah Corbutt · THE WITCH BAG · *The Witch Bag* · Seren

Gordon Day · 843 · North 30

Jane Draycott · No 3 FROM USES FOR THE THAMES · The Waterlog

Ann Drysdale · SHIBBOLETH · *Backwork* · Peterloo Poets

Carol Ann Duffy · THE MAP-WOMAN · *Feminine Gospels* · Picador

Ian Duhig · ROSARY · Poetry London

Helen Dunmore · THE COFFIN-MAKERS · *Out of the Blue* · Bloodaxe Books

Paul Farley · THE LANDING STAGE · THE SEA IN THE SEVENTEENTH CENTURY · *The Ice Age* · Picador

Gabriel Fitzmaurice · THE BOG-DEAL BOARD · The Shop

Linda France · COOKING WITH BLOOD · *The Simultaneous Dress* · Bloodaxe Books

Tom French · NIGHT DRIVE · BONNARD'S 'COFFEE' · *Touching the Bones* · The Gallery Press

John Fuller · PROLOGUE AND EPILOGUE · *Now and for a Time* · Chatto & Windus

Beatrice Garland · UNDRESSING · National Poetry Competition

Desmond Graham · CORIOLANUS · *After Shakespeare* · Flambard Press

Andrew Greig · LUCKY · *Into You* · Bloodaxe Books

Vona Groarke · FROM THE BOWER: ELM · WORLD MUSIC · *Flight* · The Gallery Press

Robert Seatter · PUMPKIN SUMMER · *Travelling to the Fish Orchards* · Seren

Jo Shapcott · HUNTINGTON CASTLE · *Tender Taxes* · Faber and Faber

Henry Shukman · HORSES AT CHRISTMAS · THE SUMMER OF SPITZ · *In Dr No's
        Garden* · Cape Poetry

George Szirtes · KEIGHLEY · *An English Apocalypse* · Bloodaxe Books

Julian Turner · THE MAGNIFICENT HISTORY OF THE ENGLISH · REPORTAGE ·
        Crossing the Outskirts · Anvil Press Poetry

Contents

Shortlisted Poems
The Forward Prize for Best Collection

Paul Farley

THE LANDING STAGE

I've got this noise in my head: background or bedrock
is the best I can do for now. I've brought you here
to see if any of this might do the trick

like the tape of a favourite song or voice, familiar
and played in the hope the sleeper will awake
from a spell. I haven't been back here for years

and it takes a while to realise we're afloat;
the gangway down to the landing-stage is steep
at low tide. I'm hoping the river's moods and play of light

might kindle a sentence, or raise you from the deep
and empty stare that gives nothing back. I've brought
you to this exact spot, better to make the leap.

You know those hostages blindfolded in a boot
who memorise each bump in the road, the scent of tarmac
where a road opens up; who retrace their lost route

through its peals and toll-gates? This is how I get it back:
in pieces, the tang of a dream you can't forget
so carry around all day. Some proof: in this photograph

I'm listening under a pram's hood; against the sea-wall
a wind whips up your hair, a bottle blonde
I must have tugged a thousand times but can't recall;

gulls blur; the superstructures of Laird's stand
over the water, the brake is fast against the pram-wheel,
a curlicue of smoke rises, and for a split-second

I guess what story you were reading there. She knows
looking up from her picture-book microcopy,
caught in a long vowel sound. Though the shutter was slow

the grey river hides its tons of cadmium and mercury.
The arteries harden and little by little the flow
stops. Oxygen-sensitive memory.

They say the deepest strata are slowest to fade,
so maybe you wander somewhere earlier, lost
in that job straight out of school, still learning to thread

the bobbin and foot, the samplers you ran off, the tests:
like a fern in a split coal, cracked open like code,
so the light of old afternoons can shine out of the past

and who knows what survives us. On that first five o'clock
in the machine-shop – the air revved up, a smell
of lint and sweat – the supervisor raised your work

and declared, 'Looks like you've done this all our life, girl…':
so a chance remark in the light of forty years back
lives on in other minds; and you had so much to tell

which makes this silence harder. I can stand here and say
anything fluently now, to a woman in a wheelchair
who read to me, who took time out of those days

that must have contained so many things – newspaper
under a maiden strung with drip-drying nappies,
kindling in the grate, buttery firelighters –

and even though this stranger knows the little good
it does, talking into the wind; that his words are gone
before you know it; that you hear only collapsed chords,

I'll tell you how corncrakes have been heard again
out on the Isle of Man; how it's being said
that salmon are jumping the Howley Weir above Warrington;

that the grey river recalls each note and will reel them off
like verb forms taught by rote. The river remembers
its whiting, fluke and mackerel well enough

and their counterpoint that sounds in the shell of our ears
and moves in from the west, that peak and trough
and roil of surf which is our cantus firmus.

THE SEA IN THE SEVENTEENTH CENTURY

God's foot upon the treadle of the loom,
the sea goes about its business.
The photogenic reefs of the Pacific
can build for an eternity before
the cameras come, the kelp-forested shelves
of cooler waters absorb the wrecks
that scour their beds, a hint of the drift-net.
Ocean life goes on as usual, though.
A pulsing, absolute state of affairs
where all our yesteryears go through the lives
we might still live. It's boring in a way,
like heaven. Good Friday, 1649:
the first elvers have gained the estuaries
of Europe; a generation of spider crabs
are wiped out by a crustacean virus;
box jellyfish are deserting the shores
of a yet-to-be uncovered continent.
You'd almost think, nature being nature,
there would be some excitement at the trace
of poison from the Severn; at one part
night soil to the billionth of Thames:
that sightings of the brass-helmeted diver
would start a murmuring that God is dead.

John Fuller

Those twenty years we lived before we met,
Long gone yet partly traced, like history,
Seem now discountable, mysterious,
Petty to be regretted as not shared,
As two paths through a thicket reach the same
Broad upland meadow with its untrod grasses
A feathery haze of red, a Corot trick
To lose the single tuft among its kind
And lead the eye to wander where the light
Has only brilliant remarks to make.

And if my own path was a thorny stumble,
Grateful to find an opening at last,
I hardly cared what opportunities
You'd had to choose between alternatives
Or where those led, or if it mattered to you.
The seeds have fallen now, the grass is flattened,
We've almost done our feasting in the sun.
Together we attend the earliest star
As to a strict instructor of our fate,
And know by now how to respect its tale.

It stands there in the evening sky, as always
Suggesting endings and continuations,
A point of closure that allows the next
Inevitable sentence to begin,
A single blast that notifies the squadrons,
The brooding horn that wakes concerted strings,
The constellations waiting for their darkness,
The heavens waiting for the world to sleep
And we to watch, as one by one the stars
Shape their cold oracles at our request.

The future and the past might well be here
If we could read them as they once were read
Two thousand years ago on terraces
Like this, in villas very much the same
Beside this restless, many-harboured sea.
And still we give them that ironic look
Which tries to make them somehow, in our vast
Belittlement, accomplices of sorts.
We introduce them, like the years themselves,
Into our shapely private narrative.

But always underneath there is this murmur
Of some lost language, almost translatable
Yet fraught with meanings never caught or shared,
Those random busy years our life escaped from,
The years I still can be resentful of
Remembering the unrememberable,
And finding them as chastening in their way
As what we neither of us know, their final
Counterpart, the matching epilogue,
The twenty years we hope we still have left.

If history has always been like this,
Shaped only by our accidental myths
And flowing anywhere (as Hardy put it:
A roadside rill after a thunderstorm,
Turned by a straw, or tiny bar of sand)
Then should we care what shape our water takes?
Where it has come from? Where it thinks it goes?
Its greatest moments, and the most surprising,
Are what we dare to give the name of love,
The meeting of our tributary streams.

Vona Groarke

FROM THE BOWER

ELM

He says that he hardly notices, that I don't look all that different
and, now that the redness is gone and the stitches are out,
you'd think everything was the way it always was. I'm glad
to hear it, but I know it's crap. His tongue says it one way,

but his hands have it another. He hasn't touched me on that side
since the op. Oh, he'll work away at the other right enough,
but he turns his head (who'd blame him) towards the wall. I do
the rest myself, running my finger, for company, round the stump.

WORLD MUSIC

Okay. Elvis is driving inland
in a black Morris Minor
and white studded shirt. What else?
He's singing, of course,

a patch-up job on 'Sweet Vale of Avoca'
and 'When they begin…' It's 1974.
He's seen it all. Even today
he's been through Keenagh,

Ballymahon, Tubberclair.
The names are getting longer
and he's flicking butts, like Hansel,
in a trail. He wants out.

But not before his head-to-head
with the Bethlehem Céilí Band
and their full-throttle version of,
of all things, 'Blue Suede Shoes'.

So just when he's coming up to our gate
I'm ready for him with my book and pen.
Nothing surprises Elvis. He throws me
half a smile and a cigarette stub

that I swoop on, almost dropping,
in the process, my crêpe-paper flag
with its red, stapled stripes
and its thirty-two pointless, tinfoil stars.

David Harsent

XIX WHO DO YOU WANT TO BE?

Who do you want to be? I think I ought to know.
If someone stood beyond me to watch this portrait grow,
backing off to size you up, then me, he might decide

there's really nothing to choose, and less to hide;
I could become you at a stroke
and open up to darkness. We stand here, toe to toe,

as I add what's yours to you: these votives and charms,
a junkyard of feather and glass and stone, any one of which
possesses the power to put you beyond harm,

as we know, bringing them, touch by touch, to a low
Chinese lacquered table just beyond your reach.
Everything here is exactly what it seems:

the down on your lip, the tuck of your dress, the slow
blade of the ceiling-fan, the window reflecting all this;
    and beyond
the window, a balcony; and beyond, a city street,

and beyond even that, an alley, a rat-run sloping to shadow,
the *via negativa* where nothing can come to good.
What if you and I were to meet

a year from now by that self-same alley, mad
for each other, just as we were, just as we ought to be, and go
hand in hand to the end, and then beyond?

Would you still have this picture of us in your head?
Would it turn out to be the last thing we ever did?
Would you be glad?

THE HARE AS WITCH ANIMAL

'I can use any one of the nine God-given portals
to slip inside the old bitch, catch
her dozing on the settle,
knees at a bawdy angle, her hand still clutching the
    bottle
then wake her and take her out
to fret their corn with mould and leave their cattle
hamstrung amid the eyebright and the vetch.

While she's stripped and whipped I go to ground,
hunkered beneath her ribs but in fine fettle
(since you ask) and alive to the cries and laughter as
    they fetch
the stool and bring her tethered to the pond
under a sudden rain of stones and spittle.

It's sink or swim for Mother Dark; I've already found
the back way out. Look, there I go at full stretch
between magic and mortal.'

Peter Porter

In the beginning was the Word,
Not just the word of God but sounds
Where Truth was clarified or blurred.
Then Rhyme and Rhythm did the rounds
And justified their jumps and joins
By glueing up our lips and loins.

Once words had freshness on their breath.
The Poet who saw first that Death
Has only one true rhyme was made
The Leader of the Boys' Brigade.
Dead languages can scan and rhyme
Like birthday cards and *Lilac Time*.

And you can carve words on a slab
Or tow them through the air by plane,
Tattoo them with a painful jab
Or hang them in a window pane.
Unlike our bodies which decay,
Words, first and last, have come to stay.

THE PHILOSOPHERS' GARDEN

If on your way to The Tomb where today
they are demonstrating how the stone was rolled away
you cross our small North London Park
and by avoiding the roller-blading children
you take a slightly longer route, you'll find
yourself skirting 'The Philosophers' Garden',
a small crepuscular fenced-off area
announcing itself proudly by so grand
a name. No dogs may enter and no children,
thereby blocking off a half of what
philosophers disdain. Tree cover is intensely green
verging on the black; flowering shrubs have left
to join the noisy world and dampness promises
a Schopenhauerian grave-light through the day.
Unlike the voices hovering here, the place
is modest rather as a Corot sighted in
a provincial gallery, and the smell
of dogshit drifts within its purlieus. 'Dog', says
someone in the Peripateia, 'a glance
back at the spirit world', and as for 'shit'
that's what they call 'detritus' if they have
to speak their native tongue. We settle down
on most uncomfortable benches while
the cursive learning we are forced to hear
drones on, so proud of its great outwardness.

From these dark lines the People's Park seems odd
and hardly plangent, with its bouncing balls,
its ice-cream haloes and injunctions to
the fainter civic courtesies. But here
the rotund ones may read the wind: they note
on Ariel's Web a spidery message – *The Rich
can't die! Dishevelled lie in swathes the souls
of the imponderent,* and *Russell's Tiger
is behind that shelf of bellarmines.*

The colder parts of sun are honoured for
their cleaner light and nothing will earn points
unless its jargon is free-standing. Poets
say they think that song is best *moll-Dur*,
but for philosophy the fastened gates
of any Major are the only truth.
Don't speak here of mutability,
or suggest that you learned evil at your family's
breast, at school or at a job – they'll paint
you in an older garden, one outgrown
by this luxurious seclusion, weaned from
the knowledgeable by Eden's balmy weather.
So now you know – it was worth the trouble
to unlock the stiff and halting gate and find
a hosed-down seat; philosophy is what
made sense at the Expulsion: it was a grid
to hang on when the nerves were sheared away.
It sat along with politics to replan Nature –
witness the leaves like helicopter blades,
the sure eclipse of sun. We feel our clothes
for dampness, start to hear the sounds our seriousness
had banished – surely those are buses straining
up the hill; that seismic shift's from trainers
in their thousands after school. Tiptoe
through the gate, rejoin the unaccountable:
our positive despair will always keep
our prisoned bodies fearful of fences.

Shortlisted Poems

Waterstone's Prize for Best First Collection

Chris Considine

THE CRUELLEST CLASS

Roofed by drizzling cloud, sheep in their sections
await their turn for judgment.

First the tall sheep: curled Teeswaters,
Bluefaced Leicesters with imperial profiles.

Spotted and spiky Jacobs proud of their lineage,
Dalesbred and Swaledales and thug-faced Texels.

Each breed has its class and peculiar
classicism, its points and pedigree.

But here at the end is a motley group
lumped together as Butchers' Lambs,

some blackheaded, some white,
some randomly speckled, slumped,

most of them, on the smirched grass
as if aware of inferiority,

moving their jaws like sullen teenagers.
This one is listlessly nibbling

the blue twine that keeps him penned
fast. Only the smallest one

cries constantly, a bleak complaint
that splits his jaw, shivers the thin grey tongue.

But even these are washed and prinked,
creamy fleeces fluffed up and faces gleaming.

Stars today and meat tomorrow.

The Lamb Auction

First, a loud wasp noise:
amplified plainsong gabble.

Inside the whitewashed room
the auctioneer sings the bidding.

Each time, the lambs in the lot
surge through swing gates

alarmed and prancing,
crosscurrents cresting each other.

Puce men in elderly suits
prod tight rumps,

send stealthy bids. It is hard to glimpse
finger-shift or twitching wrinkle.

Boot and crook skitter the bought lambs off
down concrete corridors

so light of foot they cannot stop their dance.

Tom French

NIGHT DRIVE

The closest, Mother, we have been in years
was a night drive back from Achill on our own.
Our tyres pressed their smooth cheeks to the ice,
gripping nothing, squealing, barely holding on.

Something stepped into our beam and stood there,
dumbly, ready to confront its death.
I remember your right hand in the darkness –
a white bird frightened from its fastness

in your lap, bracing yourself for the impact,
hearing you whisper '*Jesus*' under your breath,
preparing your soul for the moment of death.
Then, just as suddenly, nothing happened –

the sheep stepped back into the verge
for no reason, attracted by a clump of grass.
For days I felt the pressure of your hand on mine.
You would've led me to the next world, Mother, like a child.

Bonnard's 'Coffee'

When I heard that yarn about Pierre Bonnard
making his friend Vuillard distract the museum guard
while he produced his tubes of oils and palette knife
to touch his work up where it needed touching up

he struck me as someone who'd seized on an opportunity
to go back over his own life and correct the flaws
behind the back of the Museum Guard of Posterity,
and I wondered would he spot the difference,

if he could revisit his villa on the Boulevard Carnot
(which the city has converted into a museum since),
between the red check tablecloth in his kitchen now
and the one that features in his famous painting 'Coffee'

which was subsequently eaten to flitters by gypsy moths.
And if, by some strange twist of coincidence or fate,
the flaws in the painting he improved that day
were the first holes in the tablecloth the moths had made?

Stuart Pickford

THE BASICS

Knackered, I steal away
for a deep soak, for heat.
Soon a sing-song voice climbs the stairs – "Dad-dy?"
You crash in upon my secret.
Five years lift the waterlevel;
cramp me up the tap end.

Down both legs are bunches
of fresh purple bruises.
As sharks fin towards a boat,
I quiz you about the boys
at school, settle on football
or heroics on the monkey bars
I'd have, for your sake, stopped.

Your body I cupped in my palms
after you'd burst from that other
dark water, wet eyes swimming
on sound; a spiky alien
that came to taste the air.
There you sit, a cupped hand
juggling the balls in your scrotum.

Your gangly frame is mine:
a waist that sags a foot;
blue eyes fading into myopia;
family ears, a white cabbage
lopped in two, bolted on
with wing nuts, like Grandad's.
These just the outward signs.

As you are grown up, the bath
isn't evacuated by yellow fog
seeping. We don't jump overboard
when torpedoes break the surface.
There are no tears, tonight,
you lie back like sunbathing, skin
flushes with warmth it's hoarding.

"Can I grow a big willy?"
you ask, tugging your mouse.
"All your body will grow
into a man." This you'll gleefully
tell the neighbours – after peeling
your skin, ironing out
the sac wrinkled like a walnut.

It's time. I teach you to wash
your foreskin. You grasp the basics.
Knowing the secret, you chatter,
compare – I too have got the bit,
the purple plum. That night
reading you to sleep, you hold
your willy and suck your thumb.

Henry Shukman

HORSES AT CHRISTMAS

In our little house Creedence were singing
about the old cotton fields, the baby
was flat on his back in front of the fire,
eyes swimming with flame.
Christmas morning, and you were at church.
I thought of going to join you late,
but instead took the baby up to the horses.
Out in the field he started crying.
Maybe I should have taken him to the bath
of stone, the discipline of a saviour, the sanctuary
of hymns –
                              But the horses saved us.
To be close to them, so tough and nothing
to do with us, and their breathing all over him,
and the flaking mud on their necks
where they had rolled, and the sucking of hooves
as they walked the sodden field.
The horses with their long heads,
underwater eyes, watched us watch them.
Then they turned, drumming the field,
leaving us alone – the damp morning
all about, the soaked grass under foot,
the baby's diaphanous ears going pink in the cold
as silence bowed back to earth.

THE SUMMER OF SPITZ

I think about girls to pass the time –
a different one at each end of the pool.
                    Mark Spitz

We watched in silence as his shoulders rose
like a pair of brown dolphins from the blue
water, gleaming, spray showering off them.

Behind his black moustache, his sleek brow,
his head was full of girls. Length after length:
girls with blond hair, dark hair, red hair,

small girls, tall girls, curvy girls. Australian,
Californian girls, French and Austrian,
girls from Gambia, girls from Gabon.

We weren't surprised when one after another
the medals fell. Freestyle, butterfly, 100, 200,
relay, medley: only one silver, the rest gold.

He celebrated each girl with a flip-turn
then lunged towards the next.
And we knew he'd never let us down.

Julian Turner

THE MAGNIFICENT HISTORY OF THE ENGLISH

My aunt has racked up blade bone steak for tea,
her gravy thick with atavistic freight.
She stands in strip-light clenching and unclenching
her freckled, arthritic hands on kitchen air.

Together, we have trawled through the photo albums
and found Ida – the great aunt I remember
fluttering in her chair beside the fire
in Hitchin, frail, her hands afraid like birds.

But in these tiny snaps she's young again,
even happy-looking. Here she is with Bud –
her pet name for my aunt – her rusty, damaged
blade of a face suddenly lit from within.

She was how my aunt survived the cold
touch of her own mother who only saw her son,
who lavished love on him, the boast of Arlesey
at her bridge parties, and who gave her none.

Towards the end of Ida's album Tom
appears; his bland disguise of tennis whites
conceals his marriedness, the way he had
her in the potting shed, the fists of his knees,

and other men: the Revd. Knightly in
the bucket seat of 'the good old Morris Cowley',
tennis with doctors from the loony bin,
and Cecil Soundry shaving in his vest.

On the inside back cover Bud stands
squinting up at the sun. She holds a wand
of bracken. With her other arm she looks
for Ida who bends down to fill her hand.

My aunt carries out the bones. She locks
the door on distant memory with relief.
We both look down the long corridor, and laugh
at the fucked Turners, English as roast beef.

REPORTAGE

Later, among the rubble roads of the suburbs
where already the broken slabs were being craned,
the iron rods uncased from them like ribs
– rebuilding was in the air, a kind of season –

I was allowed to meet a small huddle of children,
some of them mute and some merely silent
as if on parade, all with the same desiccated
exhalation coming from their throats.

After spending some time with them in a classroom
they began to speak words. They hadn't wanted it,
they were still small and only wanted to meet
their parents soon, please, or scream in the park.

Further in, where gutted windows raised their eyebrows
and whole streets were sealed in with a black tar,
others played jackstraws with the finger bones
on a sticky step. They lifted their shirts to scars

thin as their smiles. They made reloading actions,
rituals to ward off a *once-upon-a-time*
when they had filled schools with shouted insults
and lusted over labels they would have killed for.

More of it, more, they said, wiping the rainwater
from unblinking eyes, watching with disinterest
the cable men in trucks, the smiling orderlies
waiting at the street end to rope them together.

Nearer the centre silence had turned on itself.
Three small girls sat on a perfect lawn
as I joined them on the grass to wait, the sun
kindly warming the back of my old shirt.

Around midnight one said: *You were expected.*
What took you so long? Sit-down-and-then-move-on,
that's what you're called, or Come-to-count-the-dead;
your kindness isn't necessary here.

Her smile broke below unclouded eyes.
It grew into a knot around her neck.
Several small skulls watched from up a tree
as if expecting something more of me.

I kicked my heels with other journalists.
I filed my copy through the ears of stone.
I was alone with those I could not tell
about the city, which is everyone.

Shortlisted Poems
The Tolman Cunard Prize for Best Single Poem

Jane Draycott

No 3 from Uses for the Thames

'Feather!' cried the Sheep...
                Lewis Carroll *Through the Looking-Glass*

The test was to dip
the needles into the dark
of the swallowing mirror

and by pulling to row
the weight of your own small self
through the silvery jam of its surface

trailing behind in your passing
your very own tale, knitted
extempore from light

and then to lift them,
feathered, ready for flight.

Ian Duhig

ROSARY

i.m.

All Billy Shiel's boats are called 'Glad Tidings'.
The last will ferry me across to Andrew Waterhouse
Where he is writing now, with an upside-down coble
For a home and an office on his own unnoticed Farne.

There, terns' eggs litter stones that are also eggs
Under the millennium party of the northern lights,
Themselves a gigantic lid of the Blinking Eye Bridge.
He'll tell me again what he told me in the Bridge Hotel,

How individual pages of the Lindisfarne Gospels,
If left too near a fire, shrink from it and start
To re-assume the shape of the calves they parted from,
And I know if I ask he'll tell me all their names.

Medbh McGuckian

SHE IS IN THE PAST, SHE HAS THIS GRACE

My mother looks at her watch,
As if to look back over the curve
Of her life, her slackening rhythms:
Nobody can know her, how she lost herself
Evening after evening in that after,
Her hourly feelings, the repetition,
Delay and failure of her labour
Of mourning. The steps space themselves
Out, the steps pass, in the mists
And hesitations of the summer,
And within a space which is doubled,
One of us has passed through the other,
Though one must count oneself three,
To figure out which of us
Has let herself be traversed.

Nothing advances, we don't move,
We don't address one another,
I haven't opened my mouth
Except for one remark,
And what remark was that?
A word which appeases the menace
Of time in us, reading as if
I were stripping the words
Of their ever-mortal high meaning.

She is in dark light, or an openness
That leads to a darkness,
Embedded in the wall
Her mono-landscape
Stays facing the sea
And the harbour activity,
Her sea-conscience being ground up

With the smooth time of the deep,
Her mourning silhouetted against
The splendour of the sea
Which is now to your left,
As violent as it is distant
From all aggressive powers
Or any embassies.

And she actively dreams
In the very long ending of this moment,
She is back in her lapping marshes,
Still walking with the infinite
Step of a prisoner, that former dimension
In which her gaze spreads itself
As a stroke without regarding you,
Making you lower your own gaze.

Who will be there,
At that moment, beside her,
When time becomes sacred,
And her voice becomes an opera,
And the solitude is removed
From her body, as if my hand
Had been held in some invisible place?

Carol Rumens

THE SUBMERGED CATHEDRAL

In memory of Phyllis Robinson

*'1 have made mysterious nature my religion…, to feel the supreme
and moving beauty of the spectacle to which Nature invites her
ephemeral guests, that is what I call prayer.'*
                                                    Claude Debussy

It's an hour before the dawn of rock 'n roll:
Music has not so far been made flesh
– Or not for a working-class girl of thirteen.
And then I watch you play, star graduate
Of James Ching and the Mathay School,
Your technique so physical, so lavish,
I'd call it, now, *l'écriture féminine*
For pianists: but in 1958
All I know is that you are what you're playing
– You're playing *La Cathédrale Engloutie*.

A camera's drawn to the concert pianist's hands,
Caressing octaves, palely capering
– Sunday 'Palladium' stuff, with Russ Conway
Or Winifred Atwell (coos from the mums and dads),
To be filed under my new word: *Philistine*.
This is art so deep it's industry:
Music as white-water, which your spine
Channels, springing arms transform. That's how
You lift and tumble these ton-weights of bell power:
I watch you, not your hands. I watch the sea,

Out of my depth, though, like *La Cathédrale*.
I mean all this to last – the 8 hours practice
Each day, hopeless devotion – and it does

– In other contexts. Oh, I bury it,
Music, and you, and all the pain of childhood,
But lumber back like a mediaeval builder
With washed-up stones (some good stone, too) and prayers,
To raise another heaven-touching marvel
On the same flood-site, watch another tide
Swagger in and demolish every bit.

After the last wreck, when I'd declared
The end of building-works on any coast,
Strange bells began to ring for me, the tone
Rubbed ordinary by forty years, but true:
Ghostly but not damned. What if the ghost
Wryly sang, 'Promises, promises?'
It was a gentle challenge, after all.
The sacred stones were myth. The tide that reared
So vengefully, hauled by the same moon,
Was myth. Not so, my common ground with you.

How we talk up the 'generation gap',
Break our necks in it, and never find
The friendly criss-cross trails of co-existence
– That gift which is to pause at one epoch,
The people of one earth. Yes, the years wear us...
But may all years be worn as you wore yours
That day we met, with teacherly compassion,
Because the body knows when the brighter mind
Rejects it, sulks like an untuned piano:
You lived in yours (it knew) like the luckiest girls.

It's hard, though, for the tired cells to sightread
Their last prélude, fingers twisting palm-ward
In search of rarer ivory, their guiding
Beat a laggard stone-deaf walking-stick.
Like Schubert's songs, off in another key
Before we can say 'swan', you were elsewhere:
And elsewhere, in a room nearby, your music.

I'd wanted you to play. I let that go.
You counted off your new pursuits, confiding
"I love the sea. I love to watch *la mer*!"

On Portrush Strand I watch it too, engrossed
Like a child beside a piano, half aware
That this, whatever 'this' may be, won't keep,
The waves themselves won't keep. But someone plays
Debussy. Something drives the bright white horses
You're not admiring now – not from these shores,
And makes them flesh, as music was, for me,
An hour before the dawn of rock 'n roll
When you, star graduate of the Mathay School,
Lifted the great bells out of the sea.

Highly Commended Poems
2002

Ann Alexander

DEAD CAT POEM

She who flowed like mercury, or mist
over silent fields,
who had seen off foxes,
terrorized hedgerows, endangered
several species of rodent,
was now sitting on death's lap
and feeling his cold fingers.

We stood and looked for signs of her
in the grey bundle we had petted and stroked
lugged and loved through the years.
But she was looking elsewhere,
untidy for the first time,
dusty and in disarray.

Strange that when we buried her
beneath a flowering bush, in the sunny place
where she loved to sit,
we could not touch her.
Scooped her up with a spade.

Simon Armitage

Chainsaw Versus the Pampas Grass

It seemed an unlikely match. All winter unplugged,
grinding its teeth in a plastic sleeve, the chainsaw swung
nose-down from a hook in the darkroom
under the hatch in the floor. When offered the can
it knocked back a quarter-pint of engine oil,
and juices ran from its joints and threads,
oozed across the guide-bar and the maker's name,
into the dry links.

From the summerhouse, still holding one last gulp
of last year's heat behind its double doors, and hung
with the weightless wreckage of wasps and flies,
moth-balled in spider's wool…
from there, I trailed the day-glo orange power-line
the length of the lawn and the garden path,
fed it out like powder from a keg, then walked
back to the socket and flicked the switch, then walked again
and coupled the saw to the flex – clipped them together.
Then dropped the safety catch, and gunned the trigger.

No gearing up or getting to speed, just an instant rage,
the rush of metal lashing out at air, connected to the main.
The chainsaw with its perfect disregard, its mood
to tangle with cloth, or jewellery, or hair.
The chainsaw with its bloody desire, its sweet tooth
for the flesh of the face and the bones underneath,
its grand plan to kick back against nail or knot
and rear up into the brain.
I let it flare, lifted it into the sun
and felt the hundred beats per second drumming in its heart,
and felt the drive-wheel gargle in its throat.

The pampas grass with its ludicrous feathers
and plumes. The pampas grass, taking the warmth and light
from cuttings and bulbs, sunning itself,
stealing the show with its footstools, cushions and tufts
and its twelve-foot spears.

This was the sledgehammer taken to crack the nut.
Probably all that was needed here was a good pull or shove,
or a pitchfork to lever it out at its base.
Overkill. I touched the blur of the blade
against the nearmost tip of a reed – it didn't exist.
I dabbed at a stalk that swooned, docked a couple of heads,
dismissed the top third of its canes with a sideways sweep
at shoulder height – this was a game.
I lifted the fringe of undergrowth, carved at the trunk –
plant-juice spat from the pipes and tubes
and dust flew out as I ripped into pockets of dark, secret
    warmth.

To clear a space to work,
I raked whatever was severed or felled or torn
towards the dead zone under the outhouse wall, to be fired.
Then cut and raked, cut and raked, till what was left
was a flat stump the size of a manhole cover or barrel lid
that wouldn't be dug with a spade or prised from the earth.
Wanting to finish things off, I took up the saw
and drove it vertically downwards into the upper roots,
but the blade became choked with soil or fouled with weeds,
or what was sliced or split somehow closed and mended
    behind,
like cutting at water or air with a knife.
I poured barbecue fluid into the patch
and threw in a match – it flamed for a bit, smoked
for a minute more, and went out. I left it at that.

In the weeks that came, new shoots like asparagus tips
sprang up from its nest, and by June
it was riding high in its saddle, wearing a new crown.
Corn in Egypt. I looked on
from the upstairs window like the midday moon.

Back below stairs on its hook, the chainsaw seethed.
I left it a year, to work through its man-made dreams,
count back across time
to what grass never knew to forget.
The seamless urge to persist was as far as it got.

Jonathan Asser

LOST IN BAYSWATER

The night a hooker took Jeff hostage,
coffee was the last thing on his mind.
'Black or white..?' said Aisha,
golden Spandex clashing with Quicktan

and purple contacts. It was the anniversary
of Britney's death, who'd flipped out of the tank
while watching *Wheel of Fortune*..., stunned,
she'd lain there on the shag pile – as a teacher

nailed the big one – and expired
when Aisha turned up with a dad of four,
whose wife was going through depression
owing to more than a fair share

of personal affronts, like gunk behind the fridge
and Post-it notes which curl instead of staying flat.
Twelve months later, video of the fatal programme
flickered. Next to it, the tank

complete with ruined castle,
deep-sea diver, plastic weed. No water.
The teacher was a man about Jeff's age and height,
a tense expression wrestling with the answer

to the puzzle Britney never had unravelled
as she'd headed into blankness
on the carpet, gills inflated, scales reflecting light
emitted from the question master's teeth.

Caroline Bird

MULTITUDE

An army of you, hiding at the back of my eyes,
on the curve of my iris, trampolining.
I'm loping again down a street
much like the one on the letter.
The one dusting itself at the foot of my bed,
steaming with commas and question marks.
Your road is claustrophobic,
when I reach your house it'll just be a straw
sucked on by sky. I have hands like slaughter,
I have blood on my chest, the left-hand side,
it's flowing like boiling red butter.
I have internal bruises too, just inside my ribs,
just below my shoulder.
I wish your house would puff away in a cloud
of transparent smoke, would leave me standing here
like a pole staring into space.
But it's getting larger with every lope I take.
The dandelions in the garden have your face,
they frown and shake their heads.
Even the dog dirt looks like you.
How come you have such a big door?
Brass handles, padlocks and chains,
an inch of barbed wire over each daffodil,
each flower and weed. I knock, hoping
for some reason, that I might answer the door myself,
and that I might be you, coming to talk it over.

Colette Bryce

THE WORD

He arrived, confused, in groups at the harbours,
walking unsteadily over the gangways;
turned up at airports, lost in the corridors,
shunted and shoved from Control to Security;
fell, blinking and bent, a live cargo
spilled from the darks of our lorries,
dirty looking, disarranged, full of lies, lies,
full of wild stories, *threats and guns and foreign wars*
or He simply appeared, as out of the ground,
as man, woman, infant, child, darkening doorways,
tugging at sleeves with *Lady, Mister, please,*
please…

There were incidents; He would ask for it
with His crazy gestures, rapid babble, swaying
His way through rush hour trains, touching people,
causing trouble, peddling guilt in the market place,
His thousand hands demanding change, flocking
in rags to the steps of the church, milking
the faithful, blocking the porch, He was chased –
but arrived in greater numbers, needs misspelt
on scraps of paper, hungry, pushy, shifty, gypsy,
not comprehending *No* for an answer. What could we do?
We turned to the word. We called to our journalists,
they heard

and hammered a word through the palms of His hands, SCAM.
They battered a word through the bones of His feet, CHEAT.
Blood from a bogus crown trickled down, ran
into His eyes and His mouth and His throat, OUT.
He gagged, but wouldn't leave.
We rounded Him up with riot police,
drove Him in vanloads out of our streets,

away from our cities, into the tomb
and slammed the door on a job well done.
We are safer now, for things have changed:
we have laws in place like a huge, immovable stone,

should He rise again.

John Burnside

History

St Andrews: West Sands; September 2001

Today
     as we flew the kites
– the sand spinning off in ribbons along the beach
and that gasoline smell from Leuchars gusting across
the golf links;
        the tide far out
and quail-grey in the distance;
            people
jogging, or stopping to watch
as the war planes cambered and turned
in the morning light –

today
    – with the news in my mind, and the muffled dread
of what may come –

        I knelt down in the sand
with Lucas
     gathering shells
and pebbles
     finding evidence of life in all this
driftwork:
     snail shells; shreds of razorfish;
smudges of weed and flesh on tideworn stone.

At times I think what makes us who we are
is neither kinship nor our given states
but something lost between the world we own
and what we dream about behind the names

on days like this
                    our lines raised in the wind
our bodies fixed and anchored to the shore

and though we are confined by property
what tethers us to gravity and light
has most to do with distance and the shapes
we find in water
                    reading from the book
of silt and tides
                    the rose or petrol blue
of jellyfish and sea anemone
combining with a child's
first nakedness.

Sometimes I am dizzy with the fear
of losing everything – the sea, the sky,
all living creatures, forests, estuaries:
we trade so much to know the virtual
we scarcely register the drift and tug
of other bodies
                    scarcely apprehend
the moment as it happens: shifts of light
and weather
                    and the quiet, local forms
of history: the fish lodged in the tide
beyond the sands;
                    the long insomnia
of ornamental carp in public parks
captive and bright
                         and hung in their own
slow-burning
            transitive gold;
                              jamjars of spawn
and sticklebacks
                    or goldfish carried home

from fairgrounds
              to the hum of radio

but this is the problem: how to be alive
in all this gazed-upon and cherished world
and do no harm

              a toddler on a beach
sifting wood and dried weed from the sand
and puzzled by the pattern on a shell

his parents on the dune slacks with a kite
plugged into the sky
              all nerve and line

patient; afraid; but still, through everything
attentive to the irredeemable.

David Constantine

LEGGER

Casting him off from the sympathetic horses
They shoved him gently into the low hole
Telling him the drift, such as it was, would help him
And that the level of the water would not rise or fall.

He went in snug as a shuttle with a lantern in the bows
About as bright as the light on a glow-worm's tail
And lay on his back the way they had said he must
And began to leg his longboat through the hill

Mile after mile, only as fast as Shanks's
And the sun came and went and the same old stars
Shifted their quarters slowly as it is fixed they will
And he continued his course out of sight of theirs

Treading the slimy ceiling in his hobnail boots
Like a living dead as though to slide the lid
He trod and trod and the heavy water
Squeezed past him with a shudder on either side.

I have had a picnic on that sunny hill
And read 'The Lady of Shalott' to a romantic girl
Hoping it would undress her and lay her down
Smiling under my shadow and my smile

And all the while those thousands of fathoms down
Under the severed ends of sinister lodes
His legs even in his dreams, even dead asleep,
Were trudging along the roof of his one and only road

Long since without even a fag end of light
Even the kindness of dumb animals long since gone from mind
Under the weight of millions of years of rock
And twenty hundred of christian humankind.

He will be a wonder when he comes out of the hill
On our side berthing in the orange water
In the old wharfs among the sunken skeletons
Of the ancient narrowboats, strange as Arthur

In his overalls and the soles of his boots and the soles
Of his feet worn through and no light in his eyes
Under the interest of our savants and our developers
Grinning with horror, rictus of the bad old days.

Sarah Corbutt

THE WITCH BAG

Remember me. I am the woman
who shook her fisted nipples at the moon,
bearing down the dark streets
that could not take her.

My face broke in two
as I ate its bright cheek,
my hands sudden as marshlight
held before me
into the dark nights that followed.

I am the woman who flew
not only in her dreams,
but remembered the spell as she woke
and hunted sighs like ticks,
dipping and turning as she went.

That woman, weightless thing,
thin as pond moss,
blacker than the pond's black bell.
She hooks its clammy limbs around her own
and sucks the water into herself.

That woman, without a world,
who goes hopping with one boot
between twilights,
a bagful of grave treasures
lost and lost again –

mask of hair, milk tooth,
heel-bone, blood-purse, name.

Gordon Day

843

May *n.* month of many days like the rest
except February
not to mention September.

may *v.* **1.** might Spielberg do another take
as long as it takes until nothing really happens?
2. *archaic* might happen only in America.

maya *n.* **1.** illusion over there.
2. reality over here.

may-apple *n.* bomb that does not explode
on impact but lies dormant waiting to be
plucked from the earth
as yellow egg-shaped fruit.

maybe *adv.* **1.** perhaps Pollock's the man
upstairs splurging red and steel-grey paint
through windows on sky-blue canvas.
2. perhaps performance art of not taking
the lift but going down with the building
ground floor only.

May-bug *n.* cockchafer in the White House
the thick-piled carpet.

May Day *n.* annual celebration of firemen
with flags excluding red.

mayday *n.* **1.** *Mid. East.* I'll always love you.
2. *N. Amer.* get me out of here.

mayfly *n.* adult of brief life
but many flying hours.

mayhem *n. N. Amer.* panic on Air Force I
circling, circling,
sky turning steel-grey,
and the President doesn't know
where he's going
where he's coming from
not to mention what day it is.

mayonnaise *n.* thick, creamy dressing up
of the unpalatable sunny-side-down.

mayor *n.* hero of the hours that suit.

mayoress *n.* **1.** mistress of mayor.
2. *archaic* wife of mayor.

maypole *n.* annual pole for walking round
adorned with ribbons and flowers
excluding red.

mayweed *n.* stinking or scentless plant
climbing number 10.

mazard *n.* Europe's sweet cherry that doesn't
make a fist with others.

maze *n.* complex arrangement of chambers
in the ears designed to puzzle those coming
up against them from the wrong side.

Ann Drysdale

The coach-works in Bradford are known far and wide,
A centre of excellence, really,
For turning vehicular fiction to fact
If requirements are specified clearly.

We'd a bloody great order not too long ago –
A bit of a triumph for Sales –
For twenty-four buses, done inside and out,
For a private contractor in Wales.

The seats were all covered in quality twill;
The exteriors shone like a dream
In Verona (a sort of a special dark green)
And Buttermilk (up-market cream).

We'd almost accomplished best part of the job
And the paintwork were gleaming and grand
Wi' twelve coats all over, sprayed on in the shop
And the coachlines all finished by hand.

There were customised logos; two dragons per bus,
Which were done in a Post Office Red,
But we had no instructions for painting the words
So we rang them to see what they said.

"We don't want to spoil a spectacular job
So we thought we'd refer it to you –
Do you want this here *kim-roo* Verona or Gold –
And will next week delivery do?"

"The word should be *Cymru*" the customer said
With a hint of a taste of a sneer.
So we sent 'em back painted C-U-M-R-Y
'cause that's how we spell *Cymru* round here.

Carol Ann Duffy

THE MAP-WOMAN

A woman's skin was a map of the town
where she'd grown from a child.
When she went out, she covered it up
with a dress, with a shawl, with a hat,
with mitts or a muff, with leggings, trousers
or jeans, with an ankle-length cloak, hooded
and fingertip-sleeved. But – birthmark, tattoo –
the A–Z street-map grew, a precise second skin,
broad if she binged, thin when she slimmed,
a precis of where to end or go back or begin.

Over her breast was the heart of the town,
from the Market Square to the Picture House
by way of St Mary's Church, a triangle
of alleys and streets and walks, her veins
like shadows below the lines of the map, the river
an artery snaking north to her neck. She knew
if you crossed the bridge at her nipple, took a left
and a right, you would come to the graves,
the grey-haired teachers of English and History,
the soldier boys, the Mayors and Councillor,

beloved mothers and wives, the nuns and priests,
their bodies fading into the earth like old print
on a page. You could sit on a wooden bench
as a wedding pair ran, ringed, from the church,
confetti skittering over the marble stones,
the big bell hammering hail from the sky, and wonder
who you would marry and how and where and when
you would die or find yourself in the coffee house
nearby, waiting for time to start, your tiny face
trapped in the window's bottle-thick glass like a fly.

And who might you see, short-cutting through
the Grove to the Square – that line there, the edge
of a fingernail pressed on her flesh – in the rain,
leaving your empty cup, to hurry on after
calling their name? When she showered, the map
gleamed on her skin, blue-black ink from a nib.
She knew you could scoot down Greengate Street,
huddling close to the High House, the sensible shops,
the Swan Hotel, till you came to the Picture House,
sat in the musty dark watching the Beatles

run for a train or Dustin Hoffman screaming
Elaine! Elaine! Elaine! or the spacemen in 2001
floating to Strauss. She sponged, soaped, scrubbed;
the prison and hospital stamped on her back,
the park neat on her belly, her navel marking the spot
where the empty bandstand stood, the river again,
heading south, clear as an operation scar,
the war memorial facing the railway station
where trains sighed on the platforms, pining
for Glasgow, London, Liverpool. She knew

you could stand on the railway bridge, waving
goodbye to strangers who stared as you vanished
into the belching steam, tasting future time
on the tip of your tongue. She knew you could run
the back way home – there it was on her thigh –
taking the southern road then cutting off to the left,
the big houses anchored behind their calm green lawns,
the jewels of conkers falling down at your feet,
then duck and dive down Nelson and Churchill
and Kipling and Milton Way until you were home.

She didn't live there now. She lived down south,
abroad, en route, up north, on a plane or train
or boat, on the road, in hotels, in the back of cabs,
on the phone; but the map was under her stockings,

under her gloves, under the soft silk scarf at her throat,
under her chiffon veil, a delicate braille. Her left knee
marked the grid of her own estate. When she knelt
she felt her father's house pressing into the bone,
heard in her head the looped soundtrack of then –
a tennis ball repeatedly thumping a wall,

an ice-cream van carrying and hurrying on, a snarl
of children's shrieks from the overgrown land
where the houses ran out. The motorway groaned
just out of sight. She knew you could hitch
from Junction 13 and knew of a girl who had not
been seen since she did; had heard of a kid who'd run
across all six lanes for a dare before he was tossed
by a lorry into the air like a doll. But the motorway
was flowing away, was a roaring river of metal
and light, cheerio, au revoir, auf wierdersehn, ciao.

She stared in the mirror as she got dressed,
both arms raised over her head, the roads
for east and west running from shoulder
to wrist, the fuzz of woodland or countryside under
each arm. Only her face was clear, her fingers
smoothing in cream, her baby-blue eyes unsure
as they looked at themselves. But her body was certain,
an inch to the mile, knew every nook and cranny,
cul-de-sac, stile, back road, high road, low road,
one-way street of her past. There it all was, back

to front in the glass. She piled on linen, satin, silk,
leather, wool, perfume and mousse and went out.
She got in a limousine. The map perspired
under her clothes. She took a plane. The map seethed
on her flesh. She spoke in a foreign tongue.
The map translated everything back to herself.
She turned out the light and a lover's hands
caressed the map in the dark room from north to south,

lost tourists wandering here and there, all fingers
and thumbs, as their map flapped in the breeze.

So one day, wondering where to go next,
she went back, drove a car for a night and a day,
till the town appeared on her left, the stale cake
of the castle crumbled up on the hill; and she hired
a room with a view and soaked in the bath.
When it grew dark, she went out, thinking
she knew the place like the back of her hand,
but something was wrong. She got lost in arcades,
in streets with new names, in precincts
and walkways, and found that what was familiar

was only facade. Back in her hotel room, she stripped
and lay on the bed. As she slept, her skin sloughed
like a snake's, the skin of her legs like stockings, silvery,
sheer, like the long gloves of the skin of her arms,
the papery camisole from her chest a perfect match
for the tissuey socks of the skin of her feet. Her sleep
peeled her, lifted a honeymoon thong from her groin,
a delicate bra of skin from her breasts, and all of it
patterned A to Z; a small cross where her parents' skulls
grinned at the dark. Her new skin showed barely a mark.

She woke and spread out the map on the floor. What
was she looking for? Her skin was her own small ghost,
a shroud to be dead in, a newspaper for old news
to be read in, gift-wrapping, litter, a suicide letter.
She left it there, dressed, checked out, got in the car.
As she drove, the town in the morning sun glittered
behind her. She ate up the miles. Her skin itched,
like a rash, like a slow burn, felt stretched, as though
it belonged to someone else. Deep in the bone
old streets tunnelled and burrowed, hunting for home.

Helen Dunmore

THE COFFIN-MAKERS

I can't say why so many coffin-makers
have come together here. Company, maybe.
More likely jealousy bites their lips
when they see another's golden coffin
where the corpse will fit like a nut.

No doubt they swap the lids about
at dead of night, scratch the silken cheeks of the wood
so when the mourners come to watch the hammer
bounce off the nails, they'll say it's no good
and in their white clothes they'll swarm
all over the coffin-maker like angry ghosts.

There's no need for it to be like this.
They could lend their tools to one another.
They could watch each other's little shrines
in case the candle goes out. Instead they blow it out
and sourly scour the insides of another cheap
deal coffin for the common man.
How many golden coffins can anyone want?

Of those who appear at the alley-end,
they prefer the advance buyers. It takes know-how
to select a coffin for yourself.
'In our family it's cancer. Allow for shrinkage.'
'Dropsy does us. Add it on to the width.'
Can a man know the shape of the wood
that will encase him? Can a woman
close her eyes and breathe in the scent of cedar?

These are the ones the coffin-makers like
to sit with by the spirit-lamp. For these they bring out
tea-plums, infuse *Silver Needle*

and drink before they do the measuring.
Time to compare wood-shavings,
rubbing their curls between the fingers. Meanwhile
man and wife from the flat upstairs
take their blue bird for a walk
to the evening park, still in its cage.

Gabriel Fitzmaurice

THE BOG-DEAL BOARD

I'd wed you, join without cow or coin
Or dowry too,
My own! my life! with your parents' consent
If it so pleased you;
I'm sick at heart that we are not,
You who make my heart to soar,
In Cashel of Munster with nothing under us
But a bog-deal board.

Walk, my love, and come with me
Away to the glen,
And you'll find shelter, fresh air by the river
And a flock bed;
Beneath the trees, beside us
The streams will rush,
The blackbird we'll have for company
And the brown song-thrush.

The love of my heart I gave you –
In secret too;
Should it happen in the course of life
That I and you
Have the holy bond between us
And the ring that's true,
Then if I saw you, love, with another,
I'd die of grief for you.

Linda France

Cooking with Blood

Last night I dreamt of Delia Smith again –
smoked buckling simmering on the horizon,
that old Doverhouse moon stuffing the dumpling
of a crackling sky. She played en papillote

for just long enough to sweat me garlicky.
After I'd peppered her liver, stuffed her goose
and dogfished her tender loins, she was pâté
in my hands. She got all mulligatawny

so I tossed her into a nine herb salad
of Hintlesham. She was my Russian herring,
my giblet stock. We danced the ossobuco;
her belly kedgeree, her breasts prosciutto.

I tongue-casseroled her ear, she was my Queen
of Puddings and wouldn't we sausage lots
of little quichelets, a platter of sprats
we'd name Béarnaise, Mortadella, Bara brith.

But when the trout hit the tabasco, it turned out
she was only pissaladière, garam
masala as a savoyard. Arrowroot.
Just another dip in love with crudités.

And I've stroganoffed with too many of them.
I chopped home to my own bloater paste and triped
myself into a carcass. No wonder I woke up
with scarlet farts, dried blood under my fingernails,

dreaming of Delia, her oxtail, again.

Beatrice Garland

Undressing

Like slipping stitches
or unmaking a bed
or rain from tiles,
they come tumbling off:
green dress, pale stockings,
loose silk – like mown grass
or blown roses,
subsiding in little heaps
and holding for a while
a faint perfume – soap,
warm skin – linking
these soft replicas of self.

And why stop there?
Why not like an animal,
a seed, a fruit, go on
to shed old layers of moult,
snakeskin, seed-husk, pelt
or hard green-walnut coat,
till all the roughnesses
of knocking age
are lost and something
soft, unshelled, unstained
emerges blinking
into open ground?

And perhaps in time
this slow undoing will arrive
at some imagined core,
some dense and green-white bud,
weightless, untouchable.

Yes. It will come,
that last let-fall of garment,
nerve, bright hair and bone –
the rest is earth,
casements of air,
close coverings of rain,
the casual sun.

Desmond Graham

Coriolanus never comes:
sometimes you see his handiwork
in *The Chronicle* – someone in hospital,
a corpse; he runs things
his way, has a way with people,
foot soldiers of his mutilate
and kill; he is a man of honour
and decision: his only vice,
as he says, is success.
Meanwhile, whole streets in Elswick
are dedicated to not talking,
not even waiting for the knock,
pensioners who rummage through the dustbins,
children who will never go to school:
that's how things are and he, for one,
just cannot understand the fuss.

Andrew Greig

LUCKY

for Lesley

Certainly I've been lucky. Always a lover
since I left home, stayed night or weekend
but never the week. This chanced
so often it must have been willed.
That one who spoke and meant it
of intimacy so tight her ribs would fit
inside mine – little wonder she was eloquent
sensing the cage I breathed within!

I don't know how it happened
but now the factor knows my name
I have the run of man's estate.
Though the river is not what it was,
the brown and silver fish still flicker,
the hills still make me rise and sweat.
In the orchard now at summer's end
sweet and bitter fruit fall alike to earth.

Lie in bed, eyes open to the dark
while her breathing shifts the sheet
back and forward tinily across my chest.
Feel them fall, the fruit of thirty years
of love and loss, truths and delusions;
feel them come home and lie
on the thick, soft ground of my life
with only the slightest of bruising.

Geoffrey Hill

FROM THE ORCHARDS OF SYON

I

Now there is no due season. Do not
mourn unduly. You have sometimes said
that I project a show more
stressful than delightful. Watch my hands
confabulate their shadowed rhetoric,
gestures of benediction; maledictions
by arrangement. For us there is
no deadline, neither for stand nor standoff.
I can prolong the act at times
to rival Augustine, this shutter
play among words, befitting
a pact with light, the contra-Faustian heist
from judgement to mercy.
I shall promote our going and coming,
as shadows, in expressive light; take
my belief, if only through a process
taxing salvation – may I proceed? –
not merely to divert with faith and fiction,
to ease peregrination, what a life!
Has it ever been staged
seriously outside Spain, I mean
La Vida es Sueño? Tell me, is this the way
to the Orchards of Syon
where I left you thinking I would return?

Selima Hill

PORTRAIT OF MY LOVER AS A GOOSE

Geese were made to paddle in small ponds
and eat warm mash
and live on citadels.
Geese were made, my darling,
to be eaten,
by candle-light.
You should have been a goose.

Clive James

Advertisements asked: "Which twin has the Toni?"
Our mothers were supposed to be non-plussed.
Dense paragraphs of technical baloney
Explained the close resemblance of the phoney
To the Expensive Perm. It worked on trust.

The barber tried to tell me the same sheila
With the same Expensive Perm was pictured twice.
He said the Toni treatment was paint-sealer
Re-bottled by a second-hand car dealer
And did to hair what strychnine did to mice.

Our mothers all survived, but not the perms.
Two hours at most the Toni bobbed and dazzled
Before the waves were back on level terms,
Limp as the spear-points of the household germs
An avalanche of Vim left looking frazzled.

Another false economy, home brew
Seethed after nightfall in the laundry copper.
Bought on the sly, the hops were left to stew
Into a mulch that grunted as it grew.
You had to sample it with an eye-dropper,

Not stir it with a stick as one mum did.
She piled housebricks on top, thinking the gas
Would have nowhere to go. Lucky she hid
Inside the house. The copper blew its lid
Like Krakatoa to emit a mass

Of foam. The laundry window bulged and broke.
The prodigy invaded the back yard.
Spreading across the lawn like evil smoke

It murdered her hydrangeas at a stroke
And long before the dawn it had set hard.

On a world scale, one hardly needs to note,
Those Aussie battlers barely had a taste
Of deprivation. Reeling from the boat
Came reffo women who had eaten goat
Only on feast days. Still, it is the waste

I think of, the long years without our men,
And only the Yanks to offer luxuries
At a price no decent woman thought of then
As one she could afford, waiting for when
The Man Himself came back from Overseas.

And then I think of those whose men did not:
My mother one of them. She who had kept
Herself for him for so long, and for what?
To creep, when I had splinters, to my cot
With tweezers and a needle while I slept?

Now comes the time I fly to sit with her
Where she lies waiting, to what end we know.
We trade our stories of the way things were,
The home brew and the perm like rabbit fur.
How sad, she says, the heart is last to go.

The heart, the heart. I still can hear it break.
She asked for nothing except his return.
To pay so great a debt, what does it take?
My books, degrees, the money that I make?
Proud of a son who never seems to learn,

She can't forget I lost my good pen-knife.
Those memories of waste do not grow dim
When you, for Occupation, write: Housewife.
Out of this world, God grant them both the life
She gave me and I had instead of him.

John Kay

LINES

Trying to argue that it isn't my fault
that Khartoum was designed in the shape
of a Union Jack is a bit of a lost cause. But,

when I say I was in heaven, stretched
on my back over the roof of the railway carriage
to Babanusa, through the desert, at night,

marvelling at the stars, and the spaces between, and
during the day; tracking the sun,
long-jumping over the line from horizon to horizon;

I'm sorry that all you hear is the bit about the one line;
and yes, I sympathise that there's only one line
because 'we' only built one line; it's our fault. And

I agree it's probably not civilised to sit on the roof of a train;
or right to blaspheme about being in Heaven, and I'm sorry
if my reference to being 'on top' was misinterpreted. But

when I tell you about the parrots on the solitary telephone
line, bouncing exotic tightrope walkers, feathers fluttering
in the dry desert wind, I'm sorry that all you hear is the bit

about the single line. And I believe you when you say it's 'our'
fault because 'we' only put up one telephone line from
north to south, I'm sure you're right. I'll have to live with it. But

I'm sorry you missed the bit about the parrots, and the desert.
Because I've never noticed the parrots sitting on telephone lines
between Bournemouth and Waterloo. I've never looked for them. And

I'd never even been on top of the train, under such a starry sky,
   in fact
I'd never been on top of the train under any sky, or been able to see
both horizons at the same time and yes, I know that's all
   'our' fault.

Roddy Lumsden

Simpatika

No one speaks more quietly than the lift girl
rising and descending in the library
at the University of Santo Tomas
whose whisper exists at one scintilla –
no more – above the effort of my silence,
whose words sound like tiny bubbles bursting.
Listen now – a stopped clock has more music,
a tray of water roars and rises higher
and yet when I lean in to choose a number,
I'm certain it is your name she is saying.

Sarah Maguire

Zaatar

for Zakaria Mohammed

Astringent, aromatic, antiseptic –
the souls of the dead
come to rest in the blooms
of this bitter herb

to haunt the bleached landscape
of limestone
of broken stones
of olive trees stricken and wasted

Incendiary – a volatile oil
can be crushed from its leaves
small pockets of scent
toughened, hirsute

Uprooted, exploded
ground under foot
its pungency rises
staining the air –

pollen like gunpowder
dust in the hand
cast over Palestine
from the mouths of stones

Note: *Zaatar is the Arabic word for thyme (*Thymus vulgaris*) and is the
plant most powerfully associated with Palestine, where it grows in profusion.*

Robert Minhinnick

The Discovery of Radioactivity

When Monsieur Bequerel returns to Paris
He takes out a key and unlocks a drawer
In his desk. Then he understands.

It is as if the black stone he had placed there
Is breathing. Something has come out of it.
The hot soul of the stone squats in the dark of the desk.

One hundred years later
I edge the Astro as far as the barbed wire:
The road ends with a warning sign

With the warning worn away.
In the prickly pear our geiger starts to percolate.
It is as if somewhere the junco, somewhere the chickadee

Were scolding us. But Daniel speaks
Our instructions. Stay here too long
And we'll give the daughters of uranium

A bedroom in our bones.
So no one lives here now.
No one will ever live here

But the desert poltergeists –
Thorium, Americium, each a wild child
Run off into the world,

Performing great deeds, performing terrible deeds,
But beyond us now, strayed forever out of reach.
Ah, Monsieur Bequerel, help us to understand.

When our sun is as small as the heart of the prickly pear
The atoms of your black stone
Will still scintillate,

Compulsive as that key you finger
In the pocket of your waistcoat,
Impatient on the journey home.

Helena Nelson

WHEN MY DAUGHTER GOES DOWN TO THE DARK

Even before she goes, she stops eating.
We're up to the neck in harvest loaves
and melons and grapes and nectarines
and she sips, sips cold bottled water,
crumbles a morsel of empty toast,
touches her lips with a hollow spoon.

She knows, of course, his fondness for bone,
desire that flares for the concave pelvis,
lust for the shaft of shoulder and shin.
And she knows he will have no telephone.

Her eyes deepen. She puts on pearls,
dresses herself darkest blue.
Shadows soften her mouth, her chin;
new frost sparkles beneath her skin.

I hold her briefly in desperate arms,
flinch at the sharpness of her frame,
say – nothing. The hardness of parting
turns all words to leaves. In my garden
I long to keep her. She moves away.
No use, she says, this dependency.

I cut back dead wood. She, down there,
pares her hands to their lonely skill,
curves to the task of claw and tendon,
bends to the banquet of seven seeds.

But she'll come back. She always comes back.
Or so she says. There are arrows like buds

in the brown beech hedge. Skulls of bulbs
sulk in the ground. Yellow, the grass,
but not quite dead.

My love, my darling, my only daughter –
all I see in the world is Winter.
I beg you to change the doom that's on us.

Listen. This business is simply a myth.
No Underworld beckons, no Hades, no Throne,
no call for you to be anyone's Queen.
If – flesh of my flesh, bone of my bone,
you can make your own story –
will you come home?

Eiléan Ní Chuilleanáin

A WAVE

When is the wave's return?
Everything is still now,
The surface is tight and crawling.

It moves as it is drawn by the future tense
Muttering like a crowd with a rumour of quarrels,
Piled over a reef of glossaries.

Withdrawing it hauled away pebbles, hammering, dumping
On open mouths, boulders flattening words.
So the words are there, but stopped. When the wave comes back

Drowning the watchman's brazier.
And the macaronic street cries,
It will flow over all the names.

Words will be there but already,
Written in the new cursive,
They waver like flourishes at the edge of a tide,

A repeating film and ripple,
Clear like thin ice, displaying
A precious mosaic of sand.

The weights are buried,
The cobbles of the woodyard
Sunk with their splinters deep as ballast.

The voice of the wave will be all
We will be expected to understand.

Alice Oswald

FROM DART

'... I jumped off the bus, I walked straight across, it was ice
now this is the real river, this is the Queen of the Dart
where it jinks down like through lawns almost'

the way I talk in my many-headed turbulence
among these modulations, this nimbus of words kept in motion
sing-calling something definitely human,

will somebody sing this riffle perfectly as the invisible river
sings it, quite different from this harsh primary
repertoire of murmurs, without any hardware

of stones and jointed sticks, one note
that rives apart the two worlds without any crossing
'I could show you a place it shallows over rocks

where the salmon flip out sometimes right onto the stones
    or they used to
and you could catch them bare-handed, now listen to this,
I was lugging this fish the size of myself,

taking the short-cut through the Abbey and up
picture it, up comes a monk and imagine
he gives me a suitcase to smuggle it out past the bailiff...'

Smuggle it under the threshold of listening
into the ark of the soul, where the invisible
clear first water, the real Dart

writhes like a black fire, smelling of fish and soil
and traces a red leaf flood mark
and catches a drift of placer gold in her cracks...

Ruth Padel

Shall I tell how she went to India
At the age of eighty
For a week in the monsoon

    Because her last unmarried son
    Was getting married to a girl
    With a mask of yellow turmeric on her face

At the shrine of Maa Markoma
In the forest where Orissa's last
Recorded human sacrifice took place?

    How this mother of mine rode a motorbike,
    Pillion, up a leopard-and-leeches path
    Through jungle at full moon,

Getting off to shove away
The sleeping buffalo,
Puddled shaves of sacred calf?

    How she who hates all frills
    Watched her feet painted scarlet henna,
    Flip-flop pattern between the toes

And backward swastikas at heel, without a murmur?
How she climbed barefoot to Shiva
Up a rock-slide – where God sat

    Cross-legged, navy blue,
    On a boulder above his cave,
    One hand forbidding anyone impure,

Or wearing leather, to come in?
How she forded Cobra River
In a hundred degrees at noon

    To reach the God's familiar – his little bull of stone,
    A pinky blaze of ribbons, bells, hibiscus –
    And, lifelong sceptic that she is,

The eyes of all the valley on her – Tribal, Hindu,
Atheist and Christian – bowed? Shall I tell how you
Laughed fondly at me for my pride

    In her? How I wait on the miracle
    Of your breath in my ear? Shall I tell
    Them? Yes. Tell that.

Dean Parkin

On the 16.04 I'm surrounded by boy-men
in baggy shorts and white T-shirts,
school kids, talking fast
about bikes and cc's and Pug's sister
who rides her mum's moped
and she's not sixteen yet.
Two girls want to know how come the boys
got seats and they didn't and six volunteers say
Sit here, you can sit here on my lap
and one does while the other nudges past me
to the window seat opposite.
She admires the view, as if
she hadn't seen it before,
while the conversation swings from Adam
who's going to be six foot three
because his brother is, to the girl on the lap
who gets a laugh when she says
she can feel something,
but not much. Ash has a massive blackhead.
My Mum does mine for 50p each!
You must be a millionaire!
And Henry Reed is a werewolf, with hair
that thick on his chest
and back. His eyebrows meet,
explains Jamie, putting his finger on his own
proud gap, while Ryan's only got
a *few* hairs on his shoulders.
Kelly shaves her legs every day and Daniel
wears Y-fronts
(because they're *comfortable*)
and did anyone know that
there are three types of pubic hair:
black, brown and ginger-haired people have…

Ssshh, tell it to everyone, I should!
Then the train begins to slow
and as it tucks neatly into the station
they are ready by the doors
pounding the button marked Open.

Tom Paulin

THE FÜHRER ON LANGUAGE

The English language
it lacks the ability to express
thoughts that surpass
the order of concrete things
– this means we Germans can think
and see more than what's square or round
but our language is damaged
by a poverty of vowel sounds
– we must do something about this

Clare Pollard

THINKING OF ENGLAND

And let the lesson to be – to be yersel's,
Ye needna fash gin it's to be ocht else.
To be yersel's – and to mak' that worth bein'...
                      Hugh MacDiarmid
                      'A Drunk Man Looks at a Thistle'

Let me take you on a journey to a foreign land...
                      William Hague

I

Dusk-light; the news tells of another train derailed,
and shoppers buying up the shops, and livestock
being herded to the chop – their chops unfit to eat –
and politicians once more putting foot to mouth.
Through my east-end window –
                      over the tangled tree,
the council houses: some sardined with children,
catering-sized gallon tubs of cooking oil empty beside their bins;
some sheltering one of the three million children still in poverty;
some sold to Thatcher's fortunate –
now worth hundreds of thousands, more,
with rents devised to make even the well-off poor –
over the kids and dogs on a hanky of grass,
the burnt-out car, the hush-hush trendy warehouse bar,
ISLAM UNITE scrawled on a wall –

a man's voice trails its skittering wail across the sky,
and all around me people are preparing to pray
to a God to whom I am one of the damned.

II

And what did our great-grandmothers taste?
Perhaps pie and mash and jellied eels, or hash, pease pudding,
cobbler, cottage pie,
                              pasties and pickled eggs.
when I was small there was still Spam and jellied ham –
semolina, parkin, treacle tart.
Why have we not stood with our mothers,
floured and flushed beside the oven door,
watching our first Yorkshire puddings:
how their globed bellies swell?
Why was this not passed daughter to daughter?
When did the passing stop?
When did we choose to steal instead
from the daughters of all those we have hated or hurt:
gnocchi, noodles, couscous, naan, falafel, jerk?
For dinner I have chicken dupiaza from a foil tray –
how fitting England's national dish is not homemade but takeaway.
Through thrift – the rent is due – I boil my own rice up,
long-grain American.

III

You're so fortunate, they would exclaim, as I took photographs
of them beside King's Chapel, or of willows washing
their hair in the Cam, *to have all of this history around you.*

England's history is medieval pogroms;
it is Elizabeth, her skin a crust of Dover-white,
loosing galleons to pillage fruits, tobacco, men.
The bulging-eyed thieves swinging to the crowd's delight
metres from Shakespeare's Globe;
                              stripping the churches;
Becket bleeding buckets on the floor;
and work-houses for the poor,

and the slave-trade; and raping the wife –
lie back and think of… crinolines, Crimea.
Missionaries hacking their one true path through the jungle.
Winston swearing: *We will fight them on the beaches!*

These people held the cargo of my genes within their blood.
Not all were good.
                But how can I be held up as accountable?
And yet, all of the good they earned, and blessed me with
brings with it blame. Today I filled a form in –
ticked *White British* with a cringe of shame.

I am educated, middle-class, housed, well.
I am fat and rich on history's hell.

IV

I remember bracken, and heather, and a gusty, gutsy
wind, and a plastic tub of windberries that filled
and emptied, its ink writing a whodunit on my face.

I remember Southport, where granny said fine ladies had once
gone to purchase linens, and the best. Catching the miniature
train down to Happy-Land, and my name in wet sand,

and my grandfather towelling the sand off my legs,
and then our picnic in the car – tinned salmon sandwiches,
a flask of tea, crosswords. A Penguin biscuit.

I remember sitting in an American bar having to squint
to read about abortion laws by the dim candlelight,
and sipping my six-dollar Cosmopolitan – with a dollar tip –

and thinking of our local; its open fire, the rain
on its windows, and you in it. Maybe on a Sunday
after a walk on the heath, and lamb with mint sauce,
and thinking how I never could leave.

V

Just finishing off the curry, when the football starts.
An England game. Satellites are readying themselves
to bounce the match around the globe,
and prove that we are not the power we were.

The crowd belts out 'God Save the Queen',
though they do not believe in God or Queen;
their strips red, white and blue –
two of these being borrowed hues; loaned colours we use
to drown out the white noise of ourselves.
We are the whitest of the white:
                                        once this meant *right* –
Christ's holy light; the opposite of night, or black –
but now it only points to lack, the blank of who we are.

Who ever celebrates St George's Day?
And did you hear the one about the Englishman...?

A friend of mine at home's a Bolton Wanderers fan:
they chant *White Army*.

VI

And then the news again, at ten –
sometimes it makes you want to pack and leave it all:

the floods, the fuel, the teacher shortage in the schools,
the bombing of Iraq, the heart attacks, long working hours
and little sex, racist police, cigarette tax, grants all axed,
three million children still in poverty,
the burnt out car, the takeaway,
the headlines about Krauts, the lager louts,
the wobbly bridge they built, the colonial guilt,
the needless pain, the rain, the rain,

the pogroms, the pink globe, the tangled tree,
the Raj, the rape, the linens,
all the endless fucking cups of tea...

but everyone speaks English now,

and sometimes, a voice trails its skittering wail across the sky,
and I feel not just gratitude, but pride.

Sheenagh Pugh

Night Nurses in the Morning

No bench in the bus shelter; they slump
against caving perspex, dragging the Silk Cut

deep into their lungs, eyes closed, holding
the moment, then letting a long breath go.

And they don't talk. Swollen ankles above
big white boat-shoes, dreams of foot-spas.

Pale pink pale green pale blue, even without
the washed-out uniforms you could tell them

from us other early-morning faces
going in, starting the day. We eye them sideways

as they fall into seats, ease their shoes off.
More pallid than colliers or snooker players,

the vampires of mercy. All their haunts lie near
this bus route: here's St Stephen's Hospice,

where folk go to die, there, the Lennox Home
for Elderly Ladies. Just round the bend,

the other granny-park, where I walked past
an open window one evening when the lilac

was out, and heard a young voice scream, over and over,
You bitch, you bitch, and another tone,

querulous and high, a complaining descant
to her theme. They both sounded desperate.

People who live by night aren't quite canny.
We let them keep things running, avoid their eyes,

resenting the way they don't seem to need us there.
What do you do, in the corners of darkness

where we sweep the inconvenient? What is it
you never say to each other on the bus?

As our faces wake, exhaustion silvers
the back of their eyes: not windows but mirrors.

Peter Reading

Soap

I.M., G.E.

Joey is outraged at Pacey's advance
but starts to question her reaction.
Henry disappoints Jen by not inviting her to his birthday,
while Tricia makes Marlon's day
and Rosa has an angry confrontation
with Fiona Morris. Gianni, on the other hand,
gets some devastating news from his solicitor.
Meanwhile, Fraser is forced to take drastic action
against his ruthless new landlord and Jamie
hits back at Billy.

              But – what's this?!:
Tad gets mad with Paul and Simone
and, before you know where you are,
Mandy visits her dad,
Joel's courting ends in calamity,
Roy is furious to find out
about Scott's underhand dealings
and Bernice questions Zoe's commitment,
so of course Geoff and Doreen
catch Jack and Vera out
and Linda tries desperately
to conceal the truth about Mike's health
even though Tad holds a grudge against Paul and Simone
and Pollard threatens to expose Scott
and the next thing you know is
Danny steams ahead with his plans
to marry the girl of his dreams,
Joe is not happy that Flick played truant,
Ashley considers a shock proposal,

Chris makes plans with Tara's money,
Zak and Cain lay down the law,
Tony is annoyed that Adam stayed the night,
Tim makes things worse for Sinbad,
Mick has a romantic proposition for Susannah,
Felicity stands her ground with Sean,
Joel struggles with his feelings for Dione
(Emily is frankly appalled),
a journalist looks for Nicky di Marco,
Dan continues to harass Melanie
which leads Steve into taking some drastic action,
Tricia realises the truth about Marlon,
Gary embarks on a holiday romance,
Darren is evicted
and the whole fucking schemozzle
ends in a welter of puke, shite and claret.

Peter Redgrove

UNDER TAKER

The gold foil lettering,
       In pine, in elm-panelled rooms,
              the colloquy of prices;
On entry from the common street
       the environment alters
              since you are entering
The ghost-train
       the first class, elm-panelled
              African snakewood salon.
A man with a sombre beard,
       a pleasant though grave expression,
              approaches like somebody
Who has seen everything.
       he will discuss everything
              in his parlour
Where a parley is laid in account
       with a third party, called dead.
              You would not have thought
That such matters could be discussed
              in that lot or plot
Between the house-agent's and the grocer's;
              they are undertakers
People who under-stand, stand up
              under this wax-polished portal
In whose cellars cosmetics are confected
       agreeable to the eye
              where the deceased
Will finish her struggle as a waxwork
       in the small broken parlours
              of rotting elm and deceased pine
Dressed as La Traviata, leaving
       a coffin-shaped doorway in the mourner,
              who is executing dead wishes

That fill up the parlour
                with a colloquy as an anaesthetic
                                that in the circumstances
Is agreeable; here is somebody
                to talk death with when most
                                avoid it, and prices
Are reachable. There are many mansions
                broken in this soil;
                                she must have a good send-off,
This is the first-class station
                gleaming with wax polish
                                and we walk up and down
The platform discussing death
                while the train waits
                                for the right moment
To steam off with shivering plumes;
                it is the funeral train – be careful
                                to get off before it leaves;
Its frigid corridors are full
                of daffodils, so bright, the sun
                                shines underground; the light
Must come from somewhere
                in this black.

Robin Robertson

Underground

At the very edge of the train's torrent,
its horizontal through-fall, you can feel it
clearing the platform's length like a piston
of grey and grey and grey,
pushing air in front of it,
pulling it behind; gone
leaving less than nothing, just that faint
pitch forward
into its pocket of loss.

Neil Rollinson

CALLIOPE

with a line from Matthew Sweeney

Now that I've left, you're on the wine,
grumbling again you've lost your touch.
I'm not surprised, I gave you my best lines
and you left them on beer mats, or just
ignored them. Now that I've gone you're tired
of work, you struggle to find that smidgen
of class, that flash of insight I always inspired.
Singing, she pedalled over the moonlit bridge.
Remember that? I gave it away in the end.
You called me a slut and a whore,
said I was never there to give you a hand.
Look at you now, pacing the floor,
your paper blank, the pencils taking fright,
and your voice calling for me in the night.

Lawrence Sail

The Pilots' Tea Dance

Everything at a slant
the diagonal shiny boards,
the spotlight's smoky shaft,
the way they move the girls
held in their chevroned arms
to the sly foxtrot, the waltz;
and the camera that peers down
as if in search of hindsight.

Out of the sun, they wave
like the summer wheat outside,
lost in the only dream
that could hope to outsing time
or the voice which knows that the field
is the world, and the reapers, angels.

Robert Seatter

Pumpkin Summer

No rain for two weeks
and the pumpkins grow rampant in the July sun:
shiny, orange footballs lolling on the earth.
The garden shrinks.

The Italian lodger sleeping in the spare room
looks dubious at their growing,
walks around the house practising the word –
pumpkin, pumpkin.

He forgets it the next day, goes out
to fuck boys in the baked Oxford meadows,
observes the pumpkin progress
with a face like guilt, eyebrows in a line.

He phones home to his papa and fidanzata:
I love it here: the colleges, the history…
yes, I miss you too. But my English
is improving – I will stay longer.

Later in the moonlight, he lies wide awake,
feels every globe swelling:
a sheen of expectation, root like a claw.
The bedroom walls shrink.

He leaves me tearfully – to go back to Milan,
his suitcases full of English Breakfast Tea;
insists on one last visit to look at the monster.
Pumpkin, pumpkin, he mouths in silence.

In another week, I cut the stalks,
lay the heavy, orange flesh on the draining board.
The lawn lies reclaimed,
tame as a living room carpet.

Jo Shapcott

HUNTINGTON CASTLE

Borders have castles which
have forgotten whatever passion
drove them to rise, though this one
glances at me with the old look.

Ivy forces into bluestone turrets
which a terrible sun makes gold
when it's not glinting behind arrow-slits
through which the verbals peer.

George Szirtes

KEIGHLEY

At night you can see the north wind as you lie
sleepless, because the net curtains bulge
with it, and the whole room seems to sigh

and billow as if the moors were about to divulge
a dreadful secret: black earth, scrub, thin grass.
The weather here is willing to indulge

its resident Heathcliffs from the deep bass
of fogged valleys or screaming tips of rock.
On a bend down Keighley way you might pass

a cannibalised Morris Minor in a state of shock,
its big end gone, its eyesockets picked bare
by scavengers, dewdrops dangling from the lock

of its open door. There is something in the air
stripping the paint away, nature perhaps
nothing more, the power concentrated there

escaping through the bleak beauty that claps
its arms around things, around trees and cars
and old men dropping ash in their own laps

in front of the TV and the latest soap stars,
with the dog by the door wanting to go out
into the wind across the becks and scars.